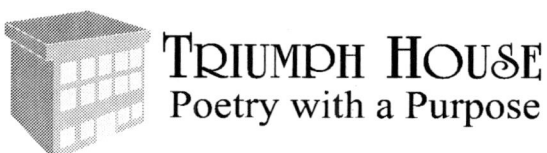

A Twist Of Fate

Edited by

CHRIS WALTON

First published in Great Britain in 1999 by
TRIUMPH HOUSE
1-2 Wainman Road, Woodston,
Peterborough, PE2 7BU
Telephone (01733) 230749

All Rights Reserved

Copyright Contributors 1998

HB ISBN 1 86161 473 X
SB ISBN 1 86161 478 0

FOREWORD

Sometimes some of the smallest of decisions we make affect our lives dramatically.

In this special anthology of creative poetry, over 120 new and established writers have come together to share the turning point that has affected their lives.

Many of the poems tell a story, others express feelings and emotions, but all are easy to relate to, reflecting true-life experiences and memories.

Together the writers have created an entertaining and enlightening collection that can be picked up and enjoyed time and time again.

Chris Walton
Editor

CONTENTS

Richest Blessings	Karen Reader	1
The Light	J Facchini	2
New-Born	Christine Clark	3
Career Change - Listening To The Voice	Anne Sanderson	4
Our Wedding Anniversary	David Sheasby	5
My Constant Companion	M Muirhead	6
I Turned A Corner	Jim Sargant	7
A Question Of Faith	Edward J Butler	8
Break Through	Jackie Hawke	9
The Turning Point Was Meeting You	Keith L Powell	10
Love Changes Everything	Christine May Nolan	11
My Turning Point	K Jones	12
A Wheelchair - For Me?	Rita Hardman	13
Roses From Heaven	Blanche Naughton	14
At What Point?	Barbara Sherlow	15
My Awakening	Janet Collinson	16
Waterloo	David Tallach	17
A Circle Of Strength	Nishani Balendra	18
I Feel . . . I Want	Abigail Bearne	19
A New Lease Of Life	Jessica Wright	20
Pippo	Raeesa Khan	21
Corners Of Life	Helen Vesey	22
Loving You	Angela Matheson	23
Reality Bites	Graham Macnab	24
The Turning Point	Jenny Proom	26
My Husband, My Best Friend	Margaret Rhodes	27
No Return	Claire Angharad	28
'Omagh' - God - Unites	Rosie Hues	29
The Love Eclipse	Chris Reckin	30
Implicit Trust	Kathleen McBurney	31
My Belief	Ian Pulford	32
A Turning Point	Jan Lingard	33
My Happiest Day	Ian Caughey	34

Title	Author	Page
The Revelation	Jean M Warren	35
Burying The Past	Wendi Harrison	36
Peaceful Haven	Freda Baxter	37
The Day I Grew Up	Shirley Thompson	38
The 21st Century	Linda Brown	39
Trust In God	A Farquharson	40
Through The Door	Elizabeth Meredith	41
Against All Odds	Allan John Mapstone	42
Solitary	Keren Osgood	43
Liverpudlian Childhood Days	Sandra Edwards	44
Round The Corner	Naomi Elisa Price	45
Church	Jean Paisley	46
Jazz Matinee 1939	Olive Gray	47
Changed By A New Spirit Birth	Ron Thomas	48
Connections	Robert Shooter	49
Blow Away The Past	Elizabeth Wilson	50
New Beginning	J P Brooks	51
Turning Point	Emma Madigan	52
Where The Heart Is	Kim Montia	53
To Gordon	Kathleen E Sanderson	54
Turning Point	Val Patten	55
The Journey	Tahira	56
Adopted	Joy Benford	57
The Day God Called	Bill Hayles	58
The Saviour's Grace	Fred Schofield	59
Hard Times	Anthony Higgins	60
Manchester To Euston	Edward Francis	61
Right? Wrong!	Kirsty Greig	62
Dawning In Medjugorje	Cynthia Beaumont	63
December 1978, First Hospital Stay	Marylène Walker	64
A Shaft Of Light	Desmond Tarrant	65
The Challenge	Reg Morris	66
Hope	Vicki Watson	67
The Day Love Asked Me To Choose	Pervin Patel	68
Teaching From Above	Cyril Maunders	69

Ode To Gracie Gander, Chublet, Dandelion, Pancake	Raymond K Evans	70
Discovery	Veronica Black	71
The Mathematician and the Writer	Dorothy Whitehall	72
Becoming A Mother	Dee Dickens	73
A Life Changing Touch	Helen M Seeley	74
Purity	J Barton	75
Searching For The Footsteps	Ann G Wallace	76
The Turning Point	Joan Taylor	78
Reborn	J G Ryder	79
God Had Something Better For Us	Winifred R Pettitt	80
A Lump Of Clay (To Those Who Are Negative To Change)	Nicholas Winn	81
Spot The Train	R S Strong	82
Turning Point	Elsie Norman	83
No Longer Invincible	Monica Evans	84
The Turning Point	Susan Glyn	85
A Wonderful Reflection	Wenn-The-Penn	86
Wheel Bliss	Maureen Atkin	87
Pathfinder	Angela Maltby	88
Solitude	Maureen Inglis-Taylor	89
Awareness	Peter J Millam	90
The Cross	John Rae Walker	91
Who Am I?	Kerry Ann Watson	92
Keep Me Turning	Felicity S Øen	94
The Day God Changed Me	Julie McKenzie	95
Hope Above	Rebecca Punter	96
Carloose, My Salvation	Marcella Pellow	97
The Class of '86	Deborah Pothen	98
That Evening	Philip Trivett	99
I Have Found A Ransom	Ebenezer Essuman	100
Vacant Basement Workroom!	Hilary Jill Robson	101
The Echo	Alison Forbes	102
I'd Really Like To Love You, Lord	Peter Spurgin	103
In My Heart	Austin Satz	104

Into The Beautiful Light Of Heaven	Andrew Duncan	105
Turn Around - Dick Whittington	A K S	106
The Handover	Eve O Lucién	108
Healing Wings	Christine Rutherford	109
The Letter	P R McDonald	110
I Am No Fool	Susan Mullinger	111
Storms	J S Elliott	112
Golden Years	Mary G Kane	113
Turning Point	J D Reeve	114
When You Came Into My Life	Caroline Amess	116
The Day I Met Him	Janet McBride	117
Lifeline	David Bramley	118
Early Morning Prayer	P Rock	119
The Day I Crossed My River And Changed My Life	Maureen Smith	120
The Turning Point	Carnela Carr	121
Paternal Pride	Kopan Mahadeva	122
A New Beginning	Claire-Lyse Sylvester	123
Villanelle For A Return	Marianne Hellwig John	124
Turning Point	M E Smith	125
My Everything	Mavis Brett	126

RICHEST BLESSINGS

In the midst of my pain I had lost the one I adored
On the fifth attempt I cried out 'Lord'
Tears there were many but hope there was none
And everything was lost before it had begun
'Why me?' 'Why this?' 'Why now?' were my wretched cries
'Won't you save a soul before it dies?'
The pain was so acute nothing could draw near it
Even I had begun to fear it
The darkness suffocating, my Saviour gone
Without Him I couldn't carry on.

In the midst of your pain I held you in my loving arms
I saw you mouth my name it meant so much more than words of charm
I washed away the tears so you could take a look
For the strength you need, it's all in my book
My dear child sometimes a loss increases a gain
Have you forgotten healing is possible in my name?
I love you, I have plans for you
All is not lost it's only just beginning
Reach for me always precious child and you're already winning.

Karen Reader

THE LIGHT
(But God opened the eyes of those called to Salvation'
1 Corinthians 1:24 (The Living Bible)

There was a little candle
I didn't know was there
Found on a dark night quite by chance
A night of deep despair.
But was it chance? - Coincidence
Or do you think, meant to be?
The light came when I needed it,
And changed the world for me.

J Facchini

NEW-BORN

I looked into a tiny face,
Deep blue eyes so full of grace.
A tiny hand curl'd round my finger.
Welcome darling little stranger.

From now on my life will be
Devoted to this child from me.
I shall protect and nurture you
Encourage you in all you do.

My life is yours
I'll take your hand.
I hope I'll always understand
And give you guidance, give you love.
My child sent from Heav'n above.

Christine Clark

CAREER CHANGE - LISTENING TO THE VOICE

Clear away the clutter of the decades,
Disengage from secondary choice,
Give the slip to human folly's blockades -
Listen for your own authentic voice.

Compromises had to be agreed to
Navigating ups-and-downs of life;
Lost in these accretions, you will need to
Cut away with careful surgeon's knife.

What about that early burning vision
Lighting up a message in the soul?
Now's the time to make a firm decision:
Set about achieving your main goal.

Happily the voice is still inside you,
And it has a lot of things to say;
When it's helped you get back in your stride, you
Fling those worn-out concepts right away.

Privileged to find this liberation,
Make sure that this time you get it right;
Years are ticking by . . . but preparation
Has been done - attainment is in sight!

Anne Sanderson

OUR WEDDING ANNIVERSARY

A wedding anniversary is such a special day
A day to remember and a day to celebrate
A day to thank each other
For times you have both shared

A day to offer a prayer
To thank God above
For the blessing of this life
Of His unfailing love.

And when the day is over
There'll be time to meditate
Remembering the vows
You've both exchanged
On your wedding day.

David Sheasby

My Constant Companion

I felt the World had forgotten me,
I could but sit and cry.
I prayed to God in Heaven above,
To let me lay down and die.
I could not find a Friend,
To stand with me side by side.
From everyone around me,
I wanted to run and hide.

Then I heard Our Father say,
'Why do you sit and weep?
Surely in your heart you know,
My Promises I'll keep?
You only have to ask Me,
I'll stand right by your side.
I'll comfort and support you,
Your foot, I'll not let slide.

Ask . . . and you will be given,
Seek . . . and you will find.
Knock . . . and the doors will open,
For Your Father . . . He is kind.'
Now the World looks brighter,
Things get better day by day.
For God is always by my side,
He's with me . . . all the way.

M Muirhead

I Turned A Corner

The day I turned a corner,
Was when I heard her say,
'For richer and for poorer,
Love honour and obey.'
My heart turned double somersaults,
My soul, it seemed, took flight,
My spirit, filled the heavens,
With iridescent light.

Before I reached that moment,
My life was, somehow, bare,
No purpose, no commitment,
In truth, I didn't care.
Each day was like the other,
What was life all about?
Full of indecision,
Mis-direction and self-doubt.

But from that very moment,
Never once have I looked back,
She gave me all the courage,
All the confidence I'd lacked,
She showed me, I was special,
This life was ours to live,
Fulfilling every moment,
She taught me how to give.

So once I'd turned that corner,
And heard her make that vow,
My life became a long straight road,
That we're still walking now.

Jim Sargant

A Question Of Faith

Your body was the victim of never-ending pain,
Horizons shrunk within a minute shell
Of agonies relentless, time and time again,
Stretched upon a cross of living hell.
Existing in a private space that I could never share
Your beauty and your spirit drained away,
And when you rendered up the ghost I could not be there,
My prayers were not enough to make you stay.
You died alone in purgatory and I'm missing you so much,
The inspiration of my life has gone,
Your knowing smile has disappeared together with your touch,
A light expunged that once forever shone.
The reason for your passing I know I'll never find
But the faith I have assures me I must wait,
I'll never understand dear heart why I was left behind
Yet to meet again I know to be our fate.
Then you may hold my hand once more and brush away my tears
So that I might once again behold your face,
No longer wracked by worldly pain or marked by worldly fears,
But blessed afresh with beauty and with grace.

Edward J Butler

Break Through

I was brought up to be a good child
Always did as I was told.
Never questioned my elders until I
became quite old.

In my teens I was obnoxious for I
knew it all you see. For I had been
taught by my elders so right I had
to be.

But then I entered my thirties and
achieved my great break-through and
then began to question most everything
I knew. It was then I started
letting go of so much useless stuff
and to see the world through different
eyes and see it all with love.

I came to see life as a journey -
one which we all must take and I
learnt to be more tolerant of every
careless mistake. It was then I began
to listen to everyone I met and not
to be judgmental and not to be too swift
in forming my opinions, for often I
was wrong!

Jackie Hawke

THE TURNING POINT WAS MEETING YOU

The turning point was meeting you
With the many good things that you do
Leading me away from wrong to right
Drinking, fighting, staying out all night
Not caring if I had a job.

The turning point was meeting you
And the rules that you set
Took me into a world I did not know
But a lot of growing-up I had to show
If I wanted to keep you.

The turning point was meeting you
Just look at us, soon we shall be three
A little one coming soon you will see
So I must do my best for him
Like praying to God for all my sins
As I bike to work each day.

Keith L Powell

LOVE CHANGES EVERYTHING

When we got married and started our life together,
We knew there'd be calm days and stormy weather,
I want you to know, how much you mean to me,
You turned my life around, you set me free,
I feel incomplete, when we are apart,
You have a strong hold over my heart,
Everything changed when we became one,
I suddenly had a friend, where before I had none,
Someone to believe in me, to love and hold me dear,
To keep me close, help me through, shield me from all fear,
You'll never know just what you've done and how you
                                        changed my life,
But I know we'll always feel the same, I'll always be your wife.

Christine Mary Nolan

MY TURNING POINT

I tell myself a Christian life I've led,
But at eighty-nine, all inhibitions shed,
I realised God moved in His mysterious way,
When all I took for granted was snatched away.
This was brought home to me all too clearly,
When my son and wife, whom I loved dearly,
Told me to Ethiopia they both were going,
As to their return, there was no knowing.
To work on TEF, the national grain,
Hopefully to prevent famine recurring again,
In the days that followed, I was bereft,
Why, I asked God, should I be left,
To cope on my own, growing sadly disenchanted,
Happier times by loneliness being supplanted.
But then it was then *God* came to my aid,
Learning to trust *Him,* and not be afraid,
To face up to life, knowing He was by my side,
My days to comfort, and steps to guide.
Five weeks spent in Ethiopia to see my son's work
On fields of TEF, realising he couldn't shirk,
God's call for help to share knowledge and expertise,
To a nation in distress, working their problems to ease,
A wonderful holiday which passed all expectations,
Extending to the *Lord* my grateful salutations.

K Jones

A WHEELCHAIR - FOR ME?
(Written from the viewpoint of a cripple in Albania)

Wheelchairs are coming from a country far away,
I've found out the time and the place and the day,
But how will I get there as I can't walk?
There's bound to be a queue because of all the talk.
I don't want to miss a great chance like this,
To get around on wheels would be absolute bliss,
My knees and hands are raw from crawling
But if I try to stand, I'm afraid of falling,
With shoes on my hands and rags round my knees -
If I start promptly, I'll be in time - oh please!

I'm feeling very weary but it's not too far now,
The church is coming nearer and I will get there somehow,
There are lots of people waiting near the gate,
I really hope there'll be one; don't say I'm too late!

Yes - they still have wheelchairs and there's one for me!
They lift me in it gently so everyone can see!
Now, at last, it's happening - as I slowly turn the wheels,
I'm really moving by myself - I can't explain how it feels!
Then I'm pushing harder and I'm rolling quite a pace,
The wind is blowing through my hair and brushing on my face,
I simply can't stop smiling and my eyes are filled with tears,
I haven't been so happy for very many years.

Someone, somewhere, has paid for these chairs,
And I will thank God daily for them in my prayers,
They do not know what they have done helping with this cause,
Allowing us the chance of life and opening up new doors.

Rita Hardman

ROSES FROM HEAVEN

Farewell to my days of happiness
Drifting down to long days of loneliness
Farewell to my sweetheart days of yesteryear
My wildest dreams are gripped with fears
My cheeks are wet with streaming tears
In my despair, I wander alone
No friendly hand, no welcome home,
I take a rest, in my lonely chair,
Wishing you were here, my life to share
I close my eyes, to rest my aching heart
To dream of days, when we were never apart
A warmth surrounds me, my strength returns
As dreams of fear, turn to dreams of delight
Surrounded by roses, on every hillside
Filled with fragrant perfumes, in Heavenly light,
Roses all around me, the petals are tipped with gold
A thornless beauty from Heaven unfolds
As I'm resting on a mossy stone
A feeling, 'I'm' not alone
A feeling of arms around my shoulder
A feeling of calm and joy surround
My sweetheart, bringing hope and love
I whisper with beating heart 'I can't live alone'
He whispers back 'You will my love
I'm always there, you are never alone.'
We turn and look across the fields of roses
The Good Shepherd is waiting there
My sweetheart pauses, one last farewell
Giving me strength and power to play my part
Then walks away with the 'Sacred Heart'
I know my love will always be there
My fears have gone, my life renewed
To face my footsteps on a 'bed of roses'
My sweetheart guiding me, to carry me through.

Blanche Naughton

AT WHAT POINT?

I am asked at what point
Was my life bettered?
- When I discovered God
From all else was I deterred?

Through my life I never
Became a parent
No, never honoured
By such a lovely event.

Can't say that anyone
Ever 'helped' as such
Yes, there were favours
But never the special touch.

Entirely different
My life directed
Away from 'the herd'
I feel as God expected.

Did I p'rhaps get married
And that's when life did glow?
- No - but when I wrote my book
- 'A beautiful long ago'.

I am the authoress
I state modestly
'Turning point' to a point
Every word - *mine* - honestly.

Barbara Sherlow

MY AWAKENING
(Psalm 121:1)

Oh, how I saw thee face to face
The eclipse veiled radiance in my place
Thine hallowed presence uplifted me . . .
Dazzled silhouette of divinity

Oh, when I saw thee face to face
A sinner repentant - full of God's grace,
Saved, tears billowed into mine eyes
Patience endureth, spirits arise.

Oh, now I see thee face to face
In unison we voyage, steps I retrace
My life transformed - to emanate thee
Thy word, infinite love for eternity.

Oh, what joy to behold thee face to face
Thy holy greatness brightens my place
Mine eyes awakened - seeking knowledge of thee
Perfect being of humanity.

I shall lift up mine eyes unto the hills:
From whence cometh my help.

Janet Collinson

WATERLOO

For five long years I had fought the tyrant,
That barrier to my academic success.
Then I stood on the brink of victory.
The last few assignments to pass my HNC in Social Science.
I arranged the folders, pens and paper on the table:
My troops to combat the coming night.

Like a general I bade them advance
To the howling inspiration of the bagpipes
As I fought to win the field piece by bloodied piece.
Another essay finished, its analysis complete:
Ever onward and upward I struggled, till the dark grew light
On a blue midsummer morn, my battle colours flying high.

The conflict was not without its casualties.
A pen dried, a faithful soldier gone to his rest.
My head drooped many a time, my bones waxed old:
But the end came, the enemy fled and scattered.
Routing my past failures in one fell swoop,
Forever stamping my mark on my own history.

David Tallach

A Circle Of Strength

They stand side by side
Unyielding, united by strength
As their son betrays his emotions
In a series of shrieks and screams,
Yes he is disabled,
The turning point in his life
Which causes people to stay away from him
As they used to stay away from the plague,
The plague which killed, maimed
And betrayed the insanity
Which this boy feels now,
Even when surrounded by a circle of strength
Built of love from his parents.
They stand united,
Cut off from the rest of the world
With its prejudices
And so called social standards,
Yet they look longingly at this world
Full of restrictions at a distance
And will someone, anyone to break
The wall of silence and join them,
But they are not surprised when no one does
As they are used to being resigned to their fate . . .
Their son.

Nishani Balendra

I Feel . . . I Want

I feel like crying but tears won't come,
I feel like screaming so loud the sound will shatter the sun.
I feel my anger bubble up inside
but I just run away and hide.
I feel the black despair running through my blood,
for no one cares enough to give an ounce of love.
I feel like just peacefully floating away,
for what have I got to live for if I stayed.
I feel all empty and alone,
as if locked away all on my own.
I feel as if nothing could be worse
as if my heart is about to burst.

I want some sunlight to touch my veins
to cure all the heartache pains.
I want someone to tell me everything's going to be alright,
instead of thinking the end's out of sight.
I want some friends I can love and trust,
instead of thinking I've had enough.
I want a future full of planned, thoughtful ambitions,
instead of failed, destructive missions.
I want someone to think of me as brave and strong,
instead of dumb and always wrong.

I feel . . . I want, like anybody else.

Abigail Bearne (16)

A New Lease Of Life

You may find this hard to believe
Just when my life changed
'Twas when my father died
I felt my life estranged

He came to give me warning
That my life would start anew
He said to me he'll guide me
In everything that I do

I couldn't take it in
Of what I was being told
He said my life would change forever
As he watched me unfold

Unfold into a woman
Of sincerity and power
Power to send to others
With love and healing from above us

I really miss you Dad
And I love you so very much
Thank you for watching over me
As I feel your gentle touch

Your warmth that surrounds me
In everything that I do
My precious darling Dad
I love you

Jessica Wright

PIPPO

Very recently,
I discovered,
That my budgie Pippo,
Is so special,
I was thinking that when he dies,
life will be so empty,
Without his tweeting,
without him,
His tweeting is a melody to my ears,
Nothing can replace him,
No other budgie is quite like him.

Raeesa Khan (11)

CORNERS OF LIFE

Life turns
for good
or bad
love is lost
very sad
purpose is my aim
I will never
be the same
education I will strive
to improve my mind
to seek and prosper
improve my dive
a corner is round
what will be afoot?
shadow of emptiness
I will shut
never, never
lose hope
positive thoughts
not soap
experiences in life
will unfold
of the stories
that are told
so don't despair
if life is down
be happy
do not frown
always someone
worse than you
be a fighter
through and through.

Helen Vesey

LOVING YOU

You measure the future,
The beginning no longer here
Slowly breaks up
The sum of a time already missing.
You fill the gap and the space
Stripping me bare,
Lonely as the travelling moon.

I am out of tune,
And time rends
All that is born in me to hope.
The voice of trees, of sea, of clouds
Echoes it to console.

Love for me lost, perfume,
Memory of a curtain
Drawn for a wounding glance.
Heavenly stigmata sign the dead.
The oceans shine with stars.
The hour spun with brow's sweat
Weaves a song in this eternal night.

For years I have been asleep
In an open cell of my earth,
On floors of seas tapestry of seaweed, foam of clouds.
Meteors fall in the unmoving air.
The blue and white globe floats
In the darkness of space.
In the still silence you are the dynamic balance
To enhance and fulfil everyone.
The innocence of the eternal kisses the earth,
And she remembers the raptures and the deadly stigmata.

Angela Matheson

REALITY BITES

It would never happen to me
All those things they talked about
Violence, police, becoming a thief
Losing my home, wife walking out

And it didn't happen to me
At least not at first
I was made to wait and see
By that craving, desperate thirst

Then it began to happen to me
Slowly, bit by bit
But still I wouldn't see
The real cause of it

Then finally it happened to me
Everything they had said
At last I came to see
Drink and I'd be dead

So I took a look at me
And everything I'd done
And everything I could be
It was clear the bottle had won

So there lay a choice with me
Accept my condition or die
It was clear what had to be
Ask them how, and stop asking why

So what remained for me
What did I have left
Plain for all to see
Spiritually bereft

But wait I still had me
A body and a mind
I could really try and be
The man I'd left behind

So that's how it is for me
I am anxiously at the start
Of something that might be
The end of a broken heart

Graham Macnab

THE TURNING POINT

The one who writes and bares the mind,
Thus frees himself of pain;
He'll find in the written word his peace,
And his soul some quiet will gain.

And all man's mind, and all time's thoughts
Will clearer be tomorrow -
For the poet's pen articulates
All fear, and pain, and sorrow.

So man must write down each day's thoughts;
Bear with him, if you can -
For each day's thoughts hide each day's dreams
While the child becomes a man.

My mind is clearer now, by far,
Since that blinding day last year,
When my life turned round, and I found the way
To exorcise my fear.

The pain and hatred that I'd felt
Each moment of my life
Started to ease, and I set out
To dissipate my strife.

And some of us will find our way,
While some sad souls will lose;
And each day hides a lonely death
For those who silence choose . . .

But they who open up the mind,
And loose the pent-up pain,
Will unimagined freedom find,
And peace of mind regain.

Jenny Proom

MY HUSBAND, MY BEST FRIEND

One grey December evening you came into my life
Just a few months later, I became your wife.
You brought me love and laughter, you showed me life was good
You've made me very happy, I guess I knew you would.
I want to thank you darling for everything you've done
You're my husband and my best friend, and you make my life such fun.

Together we raised our children through good times and through bad
Sometimes they made us happy, sometimes they made us sad.
I guess that life is like that, full of ups and downs
But you always managed to make us smile, after all the frowns.
I want to thank you darling for everything you've done
You're my husband and my best friend and you make my life such fun.

We've shared good times together, happy memories last forever
The special bond of love we have, no one will ever sever.
You're always there to help me with everything I do
I really am so lucky to have someone like you.
This rhyme is written to thank you for everything you do
My husband, my best friend, I really do love you.

Margaret Rhodes

NO RETURN

Even from the moment
I first opened the door to you
I knew that I had finally reached
The point of no return.

From that moment onwards
Nothing else has mattered to you
And as the time passes by
The more, for you, I yearn.

It feels like someone's squeezing me
Inside, so agonisingly tight
So passionate and intense
That it makes my insides squirm.

And now whenever I hear from you
- it hurts that you're so far away -
All I want is to hold you near
So softly, yet so firm.

And now that I have found you
Nothing has felt the same
Everything seems so right
At this point of no return.

Claire Angharad

'OMAGH' - GOD - UNITES

I'd lost the green of Ireland
the beauty of emerald green.
Red was all I'd be seeing
where once the green had been seen.
I saw rivers of tears to the graveyards
rivers of sorrow and grief.
Heads bowed the people were praying,
asking God to bring all relief.
God isn't a catholic or Protestant
He is God - creator of all.
With one voice the people were praying
they were one as to God they did call.
In prayer I too was united
with those on the Isle 'cross the sea.
My tears in their rivers were flowing
as in prayer I shared in their plea.
I prayed to see what I remembered
as I'd seen it so long ago.
I once saw the emerald of Ireland
know deep that the grass does still grow.
Dark deeds have drawn all together
they have something they all there can share.
For all are suffering and grieving
such pain has brought all to care.
The emerald of Ireland's returning
so many united now stand.
I shall see soon what I can remember
a rich and green pleasant land . . .

Rosie Hues

THE LOVE ECLIPSE

The love I found was the sun that lit my day.
The love I found was the moon that lit my night.
And like a strong breeze on a summer's day,
It made my heart fly like a kite.

This love like a glue - all my broken dreams could mend,
And so to this love I gave my heart, never dreaming it could end.
But this love I've now abruptly lost!
And my trusting heart has paid the cost!

For many days I've pinched myself
As tears continue to stream.
I keep on pinching in the desperate hope -
That it's all been just a bad dream.

With pleading eyes, I view the grey skies,
And the days that have now lost their light.
And I wonder how long the sun will be gone,
And the moon that embraced me by night.

Memory flashbacks - now bully my heart,
Relentlessly they tease!
There is one way to hold them back,
So I fall on bended knees.

And so I pray - please God heal my heart,
And unchain my mind from confusion.
And tell me what was real in my past,
And what was merely illusion.

But silence, is the answer I get,
To the questions that caused me to pine.
And in this silence, the message is loud,
'You'll be healed by the bandage of time.'

Chris Reckin

IMPLICIT TRUST

I remember my childhood with love and affection,
There was no need to worry or seek direction.
Nothing could spoil or penetrate my trust
In parents and sisters I loved so much.
I'm sorry I took eleven years for granted,
But the childhood bliss in me had planted,
A value of people for the rest of my life
Opening my heart to others hurting inside.
'Twas said you're an orphan when a parent dies,
I only know that I cried and cried.
When under a roof fall of coal Dad lost his life.
My childhood days had come to an end.
I had to grow up, be a responsible friend.
To a Mum so courageous in her care for five,
Including our baby boy now arrived.
His needs and ours were intertwined,
This family bonding brought peace of mind,
Until the child in the cot nearly died one night
The doctor advised a crisis would decide.
A turning point with help at hand,
Was urgently needed, in panic I ran,
In the outside porch, I prayed The Lord's Prayer,
Then I talked and cried together, to a God who cares,
The baby recovered, and I found direction,
For all of my life *I* am a committed Christian.

Kathleen McBurney

MY BELIEF

What does it mean to believe in God
And really to trust in Him?
Is it something that even I could do,
When my heart weighs a ton
With the sins I've done,
And I'm sad right up to the brim?

Can a heart black like mine be made clean?
With its past so full of grime?
When a life sunk in sin has no hope within,
Can a sinner like me
Have his heart set free
And find joy for the very first time?

Yes, thank God, this is perfectly true,
Accepting the Lord is our need,
For the bible says that our trust in Him
Means the old life is lost -
He has paid the cost;
From the burden of sin I'm freed.

'Twas for this cause alone that He came:
My path for the future He paved,
His life on the cross He traded for mine,
So forgiveness I claim
In His wondrous name
Praise the Lord that at last I'm saved!

Ian Pulford

A Turning Point

A wise friend once told me 'Your time here is brief,
Don't waste it on what makes you cry.
If the one that you love brings you nothing but grief
Just kiss him, then wave him goodbye.'

I looked at my husband of more than six years
And thought of the pain I'd endured;
The betrayals, the beatings, the trauma and tears,
A bleak future, for me, was assured.

Yet I made up excuses for his lack of loving,
Devised reasons why I had to stay.
I put up with his moods and his pushing and shoving
Life's too short to keep feeling that way.

My friend died, quiet suddenly, shaking us all,
My heart felt as if it would break.
In the light of that anguish, my problems seemed small,
So I decided on change, for her sake.

I thought of past years, all the sorrows amassing,
Packed my bags and walked out on the pain.
So thank you, my friend, for your untimely passing,
You made me start living again.

Jan Lingard

MY HAPPIEST DAY

I listened intently to the radio evangelist,
As he related that salvation could so easily be missed,
And speaking earnestly that evening on the Saviour's return
His parting challenge was one which into my heart did burn.

He said Christ for His people could return that very night,
And, with a heart gripped with fear, I realised he was right,
Knowing I must come to Jesus, and not one moment longer wait,
Lest my pleas for God's mercy should prove sadly too late.

Then kneeling down in the stillness, at my own bedside,
I looked in childlike faith to Christ the Crucified,
As I opened my heart's door, and asked the Saviour in,
Assured His precious blood would cleanse from every sin.

I'd been so wise to postpone not the decision until older,
For it was as if a heavy burden was rolled from my shoulder,
As an inexplicable peace flooded my heart and soul,
With a life broken by sin at that moment made whole.

And I still fondly remember my happiest day
When Jesus saved my soul, and washed all my sins away,
Pouring His mercy, love and grace into my every situation,
As I was made in Himself a brand new creation.

He gave my life purpose and meaning it had ne'er known before,
With those sinful inclinations now holding sway no more,
For, as an ever faithful friend, He is always right by my side
To comfort, strengthen and succour, as my Shepherd and Guide.

And what He has done in my life He can equally do for you,
So I urge and recommend you to receive now my Saviour too,
That you share the peace of mind which flows from the certainty
Your soul is safe and secure for both time and eternity.

Ian Caughey

THE REVELATION

He came to me, not suddenly, not in a flash of light,
Not in a glorious miracle, nor in a vision bright.
There was no angels' chorus, no hymns of praise were sung;
No trumpet's blast, nor crash of drums; no bells of triumph rung.
But quietly and gradually He answered unvoiced prayer,
Until I knew someone was close, to listen and to care.
His face was not revealed to me, His voice I did not hear,
But I felt His love surrounding me; I knew His presence near.

He lifted me from 'neath the waste and debris where I lay,
And by His sacrifice of blood, my sins were washed away.
He healed my wounds, restored my faith, my chains of doubt released;
He gave me new, abundant life, and showed me perfect peace.
For shallow, artificial joys no longer have I use,
For greater joys are to be found within a deeper truth.
My eyes, once blind, now have new sight; my ears,
                                        once deaf, now hear:
My crippled frame now walks upright, my heart is free from fear.

And yet it's so amazing that, through His grace alone,
To me the revelation of His wondrous love was shown.
For I had wandered far from Him, denied Him frequently,
Yet in His love and mercy, He came to search for me.
And now I often wonder how I previously survived
Without His love to comfort me, without His word to guide.
So I'll be ever grateful for His love at Calvary,
And for the revelation that He rose and lives for me.

Jean M Warren

BURYING THE PAST

I'm not bitter
I spat out one day
I just don't think it's fair
I want him to pay
He hurt me so much
He's a liar and a cheat
What goes around comes around
His destiny he'll meet
What am I saying
I thought to myself
Let bygones be bygones
Put my troubles on the shelf
I woke up and realised
The past should lie low
That was my turning point
So I just let him go
I'm happy and contented
I've begun my new life
In someone else's arms
Soon to be his wife.

Wendi Harrison

PEACEFUL HAVEN

The space surrounding my tiny home
begets no fear of moan or groan
nor stretch, nor bend in pain, no anxious inability
to tend great lawns and flower beds. Arthritic disability
spurred me to create what once was craven . . .
a peaceful haven.

To walk the space around my home
some paving and some stepping stones
interspersed with pebbles, shingled,
a 'country' plot and small rockery intermingled.
Jokingly my 'Beatles' gnomes . . . Ringo, George, John and Paul
play instruments, drumming, strumming, standing all
on my front doorstep.

Too, an ornamental nature reserve
a duck, sea shells, squirrels and, near the kerb
Scottie dog, badger, frog, owl and tortoise,
doing what my mother always taught us
to care for animals. Additionally lots
of terracotta and fancy painted pots.
Flower tubs containing variegated busy lizzies
make you dizzy.

Proudly stands a miniature conifer
in spring, summer, autumn . . . but in winter
comes indoors, decorated you will see
tiny baubles, trimmings . . . transformed into a Christmas tree.
But now in summer glow I survey my plot
thankful for the things I've got.
Forever more no need to roam beyond my little mobile home.
From all the energetics I'm unladen.
Here's my peaceful haven.

Freda Baxter

THE DAY I GREW UP

Taking one's mother for granted,
Has happened throughout the years.
Thinking she will always be there, undaunted,
She will live forever, pushing away all your fears.

On her friendship and love, you can depend,
Advice and help, are always there.
No one thinks she can be taken, it can end,
No more loving thoughts, she will share.

Never to see, the love-light in her eyes,
The warmth of her smile, you will lack.
The only love, that is genuine and true,
You sigh, 'If only I could turn the clock back.'

A child, I remained, until that sad day,
The cruellest event of my life.
You know life will never be the same again,
Without the friend who stood by you through life.

Life, as I knew it, had ended, had gone,
No going back, no return, she was free.
Life, would never be the same, I was alone,
I grew up, became the woman she knew I would be.

Shirley Thompson

THE 21ST CENTURY

The thought of next century scares me a lot
Will our climate remain cool, or will it turn hot?
Hurricanes and earthquakes could affect us all soon
The new holiday destination, a space flight to the moon

Will we all live in peace or will we be at war?
This time it could be nuclear, so much worse than before
Spaceships carrying aliens could invade our planet Earth
Whilst we reproduce in laboratories, women no longer give birth

Our diet would be of vitamins, in tablet form every day
To keep us all healthy, nourished and youthful to stay
Our homes would be run by robots, there'd be no more housework
They could be hoovering our carpets or ironing a shirt

We would no longer work in offices, we would all work from home
No more fun with the work mates, we would all work alone
We would have our own fax line and computer instead
There'd be no need to get up, we could all work from our bed

Shopping would be different, centres would no longer be seen
We'd choose what to buy from our own TV screen
Purchases would be delivered to your door within the hour
By a vehicle no longer on petrol but run on gas power

Has man got too clever, have inventors gone too far?
This century has seen space travel and the invention of the car
The 21st century predicts many more changes to give
But will it still be, a nice place to live?

Linda Brown

TRUST IN GOD

When God is in control of one's life,
you don't have to be afraid of the storms
and the floods that comes in unaware,
God will take care.
He will keep us safe, just keep on
praying and trusting and be faithful
to the end. God will help us to stand,
amid the storms of life.
Jesus promised never to leave us, He will
be with us until the end.
God is good all of the time.

A Farquharson

THROUGH THE DOOR

Forty years on the roller-coaster,
Screaming with false joy
In the high places,
Then crashing to the deafening
Darkness below.

The psychiatrist said:
'Take these pills
And you can get off.'
But it wasn't the end
Of the ride.

Someone came to the door
Of the loony self-help group.
Exuding calm and comfort.
Her morning face said,
'Hi, I'm Sheila and I suffer
From **MANIC DEPRESSION.**'

Stunned I stood there staring.
I had worked like hell
To secret it under
Piles of shaming rocks.
And here was Sheila
Bellowing it to the
Rush hour street!

I went inside,
And changed my life.

Elizabeth Meredith

AGAINST ALL ODDS

Against all odds
We battle on
From the cradle to the grave
We are very brave.
From the early morning mist
Until the red setting sun
Whether dry, or wet or cold
We carry on until day is done.
The young, not so young, and very old
Have stories of being very bold
In times of war and peace.
When we go to sleep
For us things cease
Until we wake or another day
When we can work or play.
Against all odds if things are sad
When they improve we will be glad
After all, life is not so bad.

Allan John Mapstone

SOLITARY

Sometimes
I wonder where I went wrong,
My life
The refrain of a destitute song,
My soul - lies empty,
My body - lies used,
For friendship and love are cruelly refused.
Alone in the morning, I waken from sleep,
With dreams distorted and nightmares to keep.
Who'll understand?
Who even cares?
This bitter land
And its state of affairs?
With a continuing passion for destruction and rape,
There is no utopia -
For which to escape.

Keren Osgood

LIVERPUDLIAN CHILDHOOD DAYS

I wore second-hand shoes on my feet;
My widowed mam struggled to make ends meet.
Her cherished wedding ring on Monday she regularly pawned
In the heart of Liverpool: the city where I was raised and born.

Bombed houses were my playgrounds way back then;
I grew up fast, and became a man at the tender age of ten.
Pure nostalgia floods in my mind; it only seems like yesterday
When I was a lad: in Liverpool's war-worn days.

The welfare official ensured I had breakfast at the cold school hall,
I fuelled the parlour fire by means of wood from the backyard wall.
Though I endured hardship, I'm not bitter, I'm proud and glad
As to being raised on Merseyside: when I was a lad.

The blitz on our great city was so obscene and cruel;
My morale was soon raised when the Luftwaffe bombed my school.
The game of marbles in Emily Street I often played,
Way back when I was a lad: in my Liverpudlian childhood days.

Though my juvenile innocence has ebbed and faded,
In my dreams I have repeatedly wandered through the thriving
Dockyards and along Bootle's familiar cobbled streets, back to my
Childhood home, where my mam once more would wait to greet!

Sandra Edwards

Round The Corner

Feel like
Not quite sure
In between times
I guess
Waiting for whatever's
Next in store.
Know he's got something
For me.
I can feel it in my soul
Know it's gonna be better
Than what I've ever
Tasted before.
But I don't know quite
How to open that door.
Done it before
Why does it never seem
To get easier . . . than before?
Just gotta trust and be
I know that now
It's just like way down
On how I really feel.
God, can you help her
To see.

Naomi Elisa Price

CHURCH

Without the church my childhood would have been rather stark,
I loved those Bible stories of old Noah and his Ark.

The Holy Mass in Latin reminds us of the past,
when men died in their thousands, but to God's word still held fast.

I was the Angel Gabriel when I was only five,
we knew all about our faith this was being alive.

As a child super-sensitive my feelings were quite sharp,
I always did feel something's out there but, never thought to carp.

When questioning our Teacher saying 'Guardian Angels where?'
she'd say 'Standing quite close to you just by your shoulder there.'

So, I thought that's all right then whoever is watching me,
they're welcome if they're holy, it's a lovely way to be.

In my years as an adult God is now a personal thing,
new music with its rock and roll does not make my soul sing.

Like many I have strayed away and never go to church,
Pope Innocent the 'Latin' Pope knew better than besmirch.

Our ancestors were linked by the ancient Latin way,
breaking with the past has brought us nothing but decay.

Change for the sake of change was an idea full of mirth,
next thing they will be saying 'Let's forget the Saviour's birth.'

Why not just call it Thatcher's Day let all the greed begin,
with music by the greengrocers and lemons for our gin.

Jean Paisley

JAZZ MATINEE 1939

Oh, Jazz Jamboree, you were the instrument
Of my husband's lost appointment.
Came the next day, an invitation to present
Myself as a social aid to his advancement.
Tea, in such an awesome place,
Soft music the accompaniment
Hushed voices and well-bred grace
Was just too much for one so ignorant
Of this enticing magic.

I was enthralled, my host's so humble guest.
The result, I saw too late, was tragic.
He called the leader, ordered my request.
I, fresh from Jazz, named the latest song.
And to the eyebrows raised by the sedate -
The atmosphere, so insular, so wrong
My humiliation, obvious, complete -
I stole away, this story to relate.
And my husband's comforting reaction?
'It's his loss, love, put on the gramophone,
I've got some records, let's have some action!'

Olive Gray

Changed, By A New Spirit Birth

For years I failed to find my God,
While under the spoiling tyrant's rod;
And not knowing how to break away,
Until knowledge like a birth began one day;
It was the substitution that became so clear,
To do only God's Will, not mine, I held so dear;
Then spirit freedom began flooding in,
Removing worldly darkness, and inherited sin.
My fleshly 'veil' God had taken away,
Allowing me to see clearly Satan's evil way.
God's Will is contained in his son's covenant word,
Enslavement to mosaic decrees Christ made absurd.
I obey Christ, his love, and disciplines too,
With the faith and knowledge I can actively do.

After thirty years obeying the Lord's Word,
I am confident in the new things now preferred.
Though Adam's sin is in my old flesh now and then;
Visits me less than before, which was so often.
It is written: God forgives most sins, but not all,
So I am careful not to honour dishonour, and fall.
Soundness of mind we should all learn to protect,
Bearing in mind, our flesh cannot be perfect.
Being overly righteous can be a strain on nerves,
Destroys all good towards those it wrongfully serves.
Wisdom is fine, and should always be sought;
Not like Solomon, worshipping false gods, was caught.
So faith, is a 'narrow path' in life, I chose to walk,
But is painful for those whose faith is only talk.

Ron Thomas

CONNECTIONS

Theme, silent movies into the talkies -
nostalgia, in the fifties, when saw it,
own life sadness could resolve if find keys?

Aged eight or nine, never thought film would seize
me; true - thought boredom would really hit!
Theme, silent movies into the talkies.

The movie of no-go, silent film dies,
ruined lives, drama enters my blood! Lit
own life, sadness could resolve, if find keys

taking my sadness too! My gloom does cease -
I sing and dance 'Singing in the rain' - quit
theme, silent movies into the talkies,

meant to me, mysteriously, - defies
logic, resolution in my grasp, fit
own life, sadness could resolve if find keys!

Watched film again aged fifty, fit still! Frees,
even Morecombe and Wise take off! Deep hit -
theme, silent movies into the talkies -
own life sadness could resolve if find keys.

Robert Shooter

Blow Away The Past

Many folk say they were born again
when they finally saw the 'light'
and yet for me, I felt set free
as the 'light' faded before my eyes;
no disguise would hide the truth within.
My childhood days felt utterly smothered
by illness, a sibling, the superior sort
(or so they thought), and religion.
I struggled to keep pace with classmates
missing, through sickness, so many lessons
made to feel 'not bright' and 'slow'
yet now I know the truth;
my supposed lack of concentration
my supposed lack of intelligence
were simply a lack of sugar.
If struggling with lessons was tough
struggling with 'attitudes' was worse;
the curse of being incredibly thin
the pain of being made to feel dim
the cruelty of making me feel 'odd'
made harder by strict religion;
TV on Sundays was not permitted
so classmates scoffed each Monday morn
the scorn leaving me lonely, isolated
and Sunday School, I hated, yet had to go;
today I know the truth beyond 'belief'.
My turning point - a high IQ score
nothing says more to those whom misunderstood;
I would blow away the past
if only I could.

Elizabeth Wilson

NEW BEGINNING

Down the stairs I creep at night,
Watch the creeks,
Leave off the light.
Insides all knotted, hands still shake,
No noise in case the wife's awake.
I feel for the bottle and sneak outside,
This drink I need I feel no pride.
The bottle to my lips and drink,
No thought's given to the depths I sink.
No thoughts are given to the wife and kid,
Just to this bottle I cleverly hid.
No thought to the heartache I have given,
Inside this bottle my life I live.
The booze I thought was my life and soul,
But without it now my life is whole.

J P Brooks

TURNING POINT

I am lucky to be alive
When I realise I nearly died
How did I manage to survive?
I looked back and sat and cried

I was only seven
But still too young to go to heaven
I choked on chewy
Then it went black

The next I knew I was led on my back
Then the ambulance came round the corner
My mam was crying like a mourner

She sat with her arms round my shoulder
Making sure I wouldn't get colder
I was cold and my lips were blue
I felt transparent like you could see right through

They took me to hospital
Then ran some tests
People were fussing like little pests
But when I came home I just slept

I'm now 13 but have a problem
Since that day I seem to faint
The hospital doesn't know why I do it
But now I know that there really is a God
Because I got a second chance.

Emma Madigan (13)

Where The Heart Is

The lipstick mark upon your collar
Sure, but it was mine
The scratches on your back
Were made by my nails, that was fine

True, there was no violence
Nor gambling, nor drink
But in your sleep you spoke a name
Not mine; it made me think

Kim Montia

To Gordon

We met when we were very young
I was just sixteen
You rode by our house on your racing bike
The most handsome boy I had seen.

The strangest feeling swept over me
Then a thought gave me a shove!
I was saying to myself without any doubt
You'll be the only boy I could love.

I didn't see you for a while - then
One night at our village hall dance
After I had played my two hours at the piano
It was my turn for true romance.

'Could I please have this dance?' you whispered to me
With a trembling voice I replied -
'Thank you, I would like to dance,'
Though I was feeling nervous and shaky inside.

You danced so well, and when we stopped
I was sure you were reading my mind
Because you very quietly said to me
'Good partners are hard to find!'

All of this happened a long time ago
We have just celebrated our Golden Wedding
My intuition was right when I first saw you
I knew just where we were heading.

We have seen our share of hard times most people have to bear
But there were many exciting, wonderful times as well
And if God is good and wishes it so
There will be more years about which I may tell.

Kathleen E Sanderson

Turning Point

An incident happens in your life
Which almost spells disaster;
But often it's just a turning point
And helps to improve life thereafter.
Fortunately it makes you think
And now appreciate as you ought -
No longer accepting as your right
Instead with purpose, intention and thought!

Val Patten

The Journey

Heralded the beginning of a new start
that of hopes and dreams
where happiness awaited
the sun never stopped shining
the clouds were forever

where the look of love
stole your heart

where the meeting of new companions
brought friendship close to your soul

where people pleased you
and you pleased people too!

Tahira

ADOPTED

A tiny baby
being given away
a mother's heart
broken that day
No one to care
nowhere to go
a few short moments
a child she wouldn't know
She knows she can't keep him
but it breaks her heart
when the social workers comes
to prise them apart
A desperate love
she can't deny
they take the baby
she wants to die
She prays for his life
to be filled with love
She asks God to watch him
from up above.

Joy Benford

THE DAY GOD CALLED

Ninety-two was a terrible year,
my business had gone to the wall,
all my cries fell on deaf ears,
until the day God called.
He sent me a life line from a strange source,
a pamphlet from a Christian supplier,
which introduced me to a Bible course,
and slowly my spirits rose higher.
'I renounced the demon drink,
which had poisoned my life,
and at last began to think,
towards God I now strived.'
Now I am totally in my Lord's debt,
and my life has been turned around,
but I find that God has not finished yet,
for new friends and brothers I've found.
The day God called, I was a wreck,
adrift without compass or light,
but He removed Satan's yoke from my neck,
and washed away scales from my sight.
The day God called was my turning point,
and I placed all my woes on His altar,
if your life is crumbling or out of joint,
seek the love of Christ, He will not falter.

Bill Hayles

THE SAVIOUR'S GRACE

The day did come, when all seemed lost,
My life a shambles of its former day.
I returned in pain, to your Holy Ghost,
All my money gone, and I could not pay.

I prayed to Jesus, these words I wrote,
Forgive me Jesus, for I am such a mess.
My life is over, and the world is lost,
I am helpless Lord, only you can bless.

Repent of your sins, the Redeemer said,
Forgive others, and I can set you free.
Go, forgive them all, the Redeemer said,
To give you hope, and a new life in me.

I cried out to Jesus, deep in my heart,
Washed clean by his blood, here inside.
Tears fell swiftly, from my eyes apart,
Saved by the Ghost of Christ who died.

Jesus called me, by my name that night,
God's words to me, were 'Feed my sheep.'
His voice called in the dead of night,
He gave me His word, His truth so deep.

He showed me truths, from heaven above,
We can only be saved by Jesus' blood.
Christ did show me, His righteous love,
For we are children of our Mighty God.

Fred Schofield

HARD TIMES

Having worked in an office for thirty years
Made redundant brings many fears
What does one do from now on
No more money it's all gone
Signing on at the job centre
Being over forty is rather unfair
Queues stretching a mile long
When at the desk, age is wrong
After six months sent on a training course
Seeing if one is able to ride a different horse
Motivation apparently is the key
Get out of the rut for all to see
So many are now on the sales trail
Not much money to fill the pail
But at least it's better than on the dole
Standing around all day like a flag pole
Better than any tonic, to give one a clue
Something completely different and new
Unfortunately some fall into bad crimes
At some point in our life, we fall on hard times

Anthony Higgins

Manchester To Euston

I boarded the train with time to spare,
And sauntered down the corridor, in search
Of a compartment with a corner-seat;
But it was you I found:
A chain of circumstance and chance,
Made link by interlocking link
Across eternities of time,
Had brought me to this time and place,
And brought me here to you:
And brought us both,
Upon the way to Euston,
The tingling poignancy of instant love.

But what if I'd taken a later train,
Or boarded this one at a different point -
Further down the platform, say?
Then we, dear lady,
Never should have met,
And I should not be writing this today.

Edward Francis

Right? Wrong!

A piece of paper was put in front of me.
It had on it two drawings -
One was a church,
one was a group of people.

'Now which is the church?' I was asked.
Easy, the people.
The people make up the church!
I was right.

If I took a pencil and drew,
drew the world with the pencil,
then drew people with the pencil
'Which is the world?' I ask you.

'The people,' you say.
Right? Wrong! Neither!
There was no black on the paper,
there was no yellow or colour on the paper.

Now when somebody asks you,
'Draw the world,'
draw what you see,
beauty - that is the world.

Kirsty Greig (14)

Dawning In Medjugorje

Wrapped in the cool mists of dawn,
Heart throbbing stillness, sweet isolation
An invitation to be with you, dear Lord,
To walk the path of Calvary.

Yours the sorrow, shame and agony,
Mine the sin.
You do not want my tears
Rather my repentance.

As I kneel here amongst the old,
Grey rocks of this holy hill,
The sun spins in the sky.
I know your forgiveness,
My God.

Cynthia Beaumont

DECEMBER 1978, FIRST HOSPITAL STAY
(At the start of schizophrenia)

Xmas is near.
Mothers tighten
The purse of charity,

Grandfathers look
    Forward
To more whisky.

I wait like a corridor
For walls to shut
Their doors
        On the future.

Marylène Walker

A Shaft Of Light

Have you felt the hand of God lightly laid
Upon your shoulder? The touch of grace that
Clearly says the Maker stands apart?
An echo from the mountain tops of childhood
Through the shadowed valleys of today.

Fleeting is the lightning by which we must
Divine eternity. Its memory fades
Amidst the maelstrom of traffic's melee.
But when we seem forsaken it must stand
As the key to all - to avoid a fall!

Desmond Tarrant

THE CHALLENGE

Lifetime's achievements come about in many different ways.
We may be fortunate to have help or encouragement from very early days.
There was someone who was rather ill, on medication and registered disabled.
The forces couldn't take him - a humiliation when to join friends he was not enabled.
To add to this he was accused of malingering, which to some might seem insensitive.
And yet it was to turn his whole life around to decide he'd so much to give.
Discarding the medication, and determined to overcome the condition.
He settled for a life of discomfort and often pain, achieving much - it was a transition.
And so he continued for at least 40 years without the prescribed medication.
Not giving a thought to what inspired it, where there could have been a strained relation.
In fact, he's ever grateful for what was perhaps an uncalled for remark.
For often there is a need to spur someone to make a decision, they need a spark.
This friend went through life as a contractor, a supervisor, and a sole proprietor.
Until at the age of 70 action proved him not indestructible and advice to take care is given more and more.
There is a moral here - what is it that divides the ones who have no conscience and think the world owes them a living?
When this fellow still feels guilty that there is so little time left to achieve and enjoy the pleasure there is in giving.

Reg Morris

HOPE

Life is full of ups and downs,
mine was full of downs,
I would drown myself in self pity,
and tell myself help wasn't around.

Depression was a forthcoming fear,
I hated my life and the world,
I felt that bad things only happened to me,
until I awoke and learned.

In the beginning books were my turning point,
stories to which I could escape,
but once I finished reading the last page,
I ran out of my barricade.

Then I realised the truth in my head,
life is only what you make it,
I went out and found a job,
and now I feel I have made it.

The whole world seems much brighter,
my heart holds so much hope,
I now do things I could never do,
I've even found someone to love.

Nothing in this world can hold me down,
nothing can ever take me back,
I am a happy, outgoing person
and I now feel I'm on the right track.

Vicki Watson

THE DAY LOVE ASKED ME CHOOSE

I ventured into the night with a granite fist
full of loneliness and expected hope.
Mothered by the existence of a pure knight
compelling himself to be 'love'.
He cloaked and caressed me with an encore
of memories called by his name.
His love shone reflected upon my reflection of
love, battered but not dead.
He asked 'Love me'
'Love is everlasting and denying me would
be shameless - death is inevitable - love is real.'
I answered without awe or hesitation
'I love *love*.'
He replied
'Yes - love me - I am human too.'

Pervin Patel

TEACHING FROM ABOVE

Oh Father in Your wisdom,
You showed me the way,
There is a time for sorrow,
There is a time to pray.

And in Your great wisdom,
You chose a path for me,
One which I will follow Lord,
And loyal I will be.

You sent Your Son down to this earth,
To teach us right from wrong,
Then you took Him back again,
Knowing we'd go along.

I try to follow Your teaching Lord,
Sometimes I fall away,
But then I hear Your gentle voice,
Turn back my son you say.

So sometimes if I'm wrong my Lord,
I know You'll put me right,
When You walk beside me Lord,
I know I'll win the fight.

Cyril Maunders

ODE TO GRACIE GANDER, CHUBLET, DANDELION, PANCAKE

My little Grace, my happy face,
shining eyes of china blue.
A button nose, that daddy chose,
and lips that Mummy drew.

Like swaying grasses, those long lashes,
in a summer breeze.
Pink petal ears, an angel's smile
and, oh! Those chubby knees!

That fluffy hair, makes me laugh,
just like a dandelion clock.
When it's cut, I'd like a lock,
to keep in Grandpa's book.

Grandma calls you Gander,
it's her pet name you see.
'Cos you can be a little goose,
when you want to be.

I sometimes call you Chublet,
Pancake and other names.
But for that, it's fair you know,
it's your Daddy who's to blame.

My little Grace, my sunny face,
brightens up my day
Before I close, just one more thing,
can't wait to hear you say;
'Hello Grandpa! Can I play . . . ?'

Raymond K Evans

DISCOVERY

A real turning point came for me in my life, when I discovered a new delight.

How to open my heart and let in the light, as quite by accident I began to write.

At that time I couldn't know, just how easy words would flow.

Starting out as a labour of love, my inspiration seemed to come from heaven above.

It's a lovely way of expressing my feelings and emotions, as well as my funny or romantic notions.

Without any trouble it helps me to unwind, and I soon forgot problems I had on my mind.

As I switch off my worries I begin to recall, how many good things I have after all.

Soon I am happily writing away, and realise that I really have had a good day.

This is my time to visit the place I love best, and count the gifts with which I am blessed.

Veronica Black

THE MATHEMATICIAN AND THE WRITER

As a small child, I could always,
Add up quicker than anyone in my house.
My parents were so proud of me - playing
Counting games - not sitting there like a mouse.

I went to school and yes you've guessed,
Numbers made me top of the class.
With them I had no problem - Grandma would look
At me and say 'By she's a clever lass.'

Off I went to college and a teacher I became,
The lessons children most enjoyed with me,
Were multiply, divide, add and take-away.
I tried to enthuse them you see.

Eventually, I became a head teacher and,
Into our school she came;
Jean the mature student - then I knew for sure,
She was a wizard at the mathematics game.

Three and one hundred applied for the post,
When the vacancy arose in our school.
I knew who would be perfect for all of us,
Yes - Jean of course - I was no fool.

She changed my life completely,
She took mathematics to the heights.
Reading and writing overcame me,
On these I began to set my sights.

The school was such a huge success,
She certainly made my load lighter.
Now both retired, we are still great friends,
The Mathematician and the Writer.

Dorothy Whitehall

BECOMING A MOTHER

I feel a little flicker,
I wonder what it is?
I grow a little bigger,
Now I've lost my figure.
I'm growing even more,
And feel kick number four.
It moves around inside me,
Now I'm getting excited.
Now the time is near,
I want my partner here.
The pain is getting stronger,
I can't wait any longer.
The head is nearly here,
So 'Puff and pant my dear.'
I give another push,
And it came out in a gush.
I'm glad it's over now,
A beautiful little girl.
I think I'll name her Connie,
Because she is small and bonnie.

Dee Dickens

A Life Changing Touch

Once more, Lord,
I have felt Your Touch -
Gentle as summer's breeze
Yet dynamic as a rushing wind;
Light as a single snowflake
Yet powerful as an avalanche.
For You have reached Your finger
Deep into my life.
In one moment of secret communion
You have worked a radical change,
That a lifetime of fiercest struggling
Could never have resolved.
Once more, Lord,
I have felt Your Touch,
As sure as spring bursts from winter
And morning's sun banishes night,
And I know, with joy, I *know* -
The time for singing has come.

Helen M Seeley

PURITY

In your purity be the virgin, giver of love,
Smiling, your beauty heralds the dove
Of peace, of grace, tranquillity and calm,
A faith, trust, no love would harm.

In my garden of roses, deep carmine their hue,
Their silken petals, hung heavy of morning dew,
Unhindered they bloom, touched lightly, caressed,
Their perfume lingers, in purity love blessed.

Purity of love, in warmth of your touch,
In your world anew love demands much,
Waste no thought, your life will stay,
No moment of time, for you delay.

Let no one of my cloak dare masquerade,
Portend of love, their pious hope parade,
For my love which is yours, be no small thing
Sanctity of angels, their purity of love will bring.

J Barton

SEARCHING FOR THE FOOTSTEPS

In Israel land of the chosen,
I undertook a searching of the soul,
There in the barren desert,
Under the scorching sun,
With nature I strived to become one,
To feel the very heart of this land,
To clasp at the roots of all that I had read,
To reaffirm my beliefs,
In the midst of it all,
Here at the very essence I searched for my God,

I imagined the Biblical characters,
Tried to set them in the midst of it all,
Waiting on Moses and the Exodus,
Would their wanderings,
Have taken them on this route,
To be lost I could imagine that,
Miles of arid land,
What mysteries,
Lie within these grains of sand,
Perchance Jesus' feet may have passed this way,

Footsteps in the sand,
That wonderful verse many times I have read,
We cannot see the imprints made or left behind,
Yet each grain is numbered,
For our God placed them there,
And what once was though now obscure,
Cannot be erased,
Indelible memories exist,
The essence of all that is,
Cast by the Creator,

I too have been carried when needed,
When the grains of life,
Bore heavy upon my shoulders,
When in that desolate landscape,
I was weary lips parched and dry,
And I lost my way going round in circles,
When in my own Exodus I escaped,
Wandering aimlessly,
Then as now the Lord found me,
And in the stillness of the desert my thirst was quenched.

Ann G Wallace

THE TURNING POINT

The turning point in my life
Came when there was holly and mistletoe
Lights and decorations, children's faces all aglow
Sense of expectation and merriment did show
A very special and memorable experience
That happened to me nearly a year ago.

A perfect time of the year
For something wonderful to start
This was the time I began to write
Poetry did flow from inside my heart
Filling me with amazement and delight
With excitement I'd carry a pen everywhere
That radiance still lingers there.

Never thought I would achieve any success
Oh but this year has brought happiness
Faith now in heart and mind
What better could I hope to find
It must have been the time was ripe
For the turning point in my life.

Joan Taylor

REBORN

On August 11 '94
His heart torn from inside,
The old Jim whom I thought I knew
Gave up, laid down and died.

The tortured soul that could not speak
Emotionally of yore,
Departed from his body
And dwelt in him no more.

The one who hurt his loved ones
Would never be agin'
For resentment turned to hatred
Was banished from within.

This mental shock, this trauma,
Had only just begun,
Yet as a phoenix from the ashes,
Hope eternal had been sprung.

Amidst the tears and chaos,
Debris like falling rain,
His twisted mind broke free and
Gave him clarity again.

A new and wondrous spirit
Filled the void left by his soul,
And gave to him the gift of love
With which to make him whole.

A new man thus was born that day,
A better man indeed.
Who'd strive to please his loved ones
In thought, and word and deed.

J G Ryder

God Had Something Better For Us

We sat in the park and wept,
My young twin sons and I.
Why were we so sorrowful?
What had made us cry?

We'd been turned out of our church -
A church we had grown to love.
The lies they told about us
Were known by God above.

We went to another town
And joined the worship there.
We weren't wanted there either
As, with many outside the church, the gospel we did share.

We tried again, in another town,
But soon were told to go.
Our clothes were just not posh enough,
We wept, with deepest woe.

But, God must have brought us out, we found,
As He soon provided a hall.
The children flocked in to worship
And were welcomed, one and all.

The young folk came to my home as well
And loved to sing inside,
Around my old piano,
To Jesus, their Saviour and Guide.

I'm eighty now and can't do so much,
But I've done voluntary work over forty years.
I think of what the Lord did for us,
After banished in sorrow and tears.

There are over 1400 children, awaiting papers from me,
So I try to keep on walking, to get to the children, you see.

Winifred R Pettitt

A Lump Of Clay (To Those Who Are Negative To Change)

My life was like a lump of clay
Flung down upon a potter's wheel,
It used to spin around all day
Because I never used to feel
The inclination or desire
To take advantage of my lot;
Life slipped me by,
I'd seldom try
To make a model or a pot

Or if I did it fell apart,
Became misshapen or uncoiled;
I didn't have the skill or heart
To mend the many pots I spoiled;
But then I learnt I had to fire
Each pot I made to give me scope
To rearrange
My life, and change
The way I lived to give me hope.

Now every opportunity
That comes along to help improve
My life, I take and carefully
I mould and shape each day to prove
A change in living can inspire
The quality of life at best:
Although I've found
Life spins around,
A change is better than a rest!

Nicholas Winn

SPOT THE TRAIN
(Ode to my AA sponsor)

Stop the train, I want to get off,
I think this is my station,
I bought a ticket for a one-way trip,
But I am changing the destination.
As the engineer I stoked the fire,
And built up a head of steam,
Then I lost control, as on a collision course,
This runaway train did scream.
This whistle blew, the wheels went around,
Faster and faster still,
As my life outside went flashing by,
I laughed and drank my fill,
But the brakes had failed on my one-way train,
It was now controlling me,
Still I shovelled fuel to feed the fire,
Resigned to my destiny.
Signals and points went unobeyed,
As I neared the final bend,
Then a 'guard' appeared and took my arm,
And said he was my friend,
He stood by me on the fire plate,
And slowed the train right down,
And when the train had come to halt,
He helped me to the ground,
He had stopped the train, and let me off,
He knew this was my station,
I had bought a ticket for a one-way trip,
But he has changed my destination.

R S Strong

TURNING POINT

Very early teens, outside my home
Stood on the bridge, beside the sandy lane.
Rainwater smoothly ran in evening gloom,
As twilight gathered, but how to explain
When daylight fades and shadows come
That a fear of darkness grips the brain.

I looked behind me to the sand lane bend,
Already dark, become a hidden threat,
And thought 'This fear has got to end,
I must walk round that corner without fret,
Challenge the dark, whatever it may send
Or I shall dread it to the bitter end.'

I clenched my hands and then set out to meet
'The hidden things of darkness' waiting there.
I reached the corner, ready fear to greet
But nothing happened, only pleasure where
'Peep-Boing' stars dodged tree tops. The neat
Hedgerows stood still and I walked free of care.

Elsie Norman

No Longer Invincible

My friend who's driving screams
As the crash barrier approaches
But there's no way we'll hit it
They always save the world
With only a few seconds spare
We'll stop inches short
This is a game or a film
- I'm calm
My friend's still screaming
We're facing on-coming traffic
There's a dent in the barrier
And it's deep
As we're pulled from the car
I look around, I'm still alive
Older and no longer invincible
A couple of 'ifs' it would not have occurred
Several more, we'd be dead
Life isn't a game though it ends just as soon
It's time to make mine worthwhile
I can appreciate things I once ignored
My smile is really sincere
We could have been killed
But somehow we were saved
Now my life's going to change.

Monica Evans

THE TURNING POINT

Going Up

You go up and *up* with a fierce joy that's new.
Excitement growing as you tread and tread
a path so steep it seems to scrape your face.
The whole great mountain seeming part of you,
holding you with its strength, forcing the pace
until you struggle up and reach the crown,
and find there's only sky over your head.

Coming Down

No wonder you lie there and clutch the summit.
You know it's always harder coming down,
to keep your footing as you slide and plummet.
There's no more hand-hold; you can't see your heel.
You toil on when you're tired and luck's run out.
It's fear now, not adventure that you feel.
You wonder why you climbed: - *what life's about.*

It's only then that you can see the view.

Susan Glyn

A Wonderful Reflection

The sunrise on the ocean, one of nature's enchanting sights,
a sea of rippling reflections, resembling a mass of fairy lights.
With the tranquil sound of water, as it ebbs across the shore,
giving a feeling of great pleasure, one could ask for nothing more.

As I continued walking, I could sense something in the air,
I did not seem to be alone, yet no one else was there,
'twas if I was being guided, by a strange spirit on the beach,
to a place I'd never been, but one place I had to reach.

The more I walked I wondered, 'Who could be my guiding hand?'
as I looked behind me, there were no other footprints in the sand,
Had I felt the hand of God, was it His way of guiding me,
to this place along the shore, as I strolled beside the sea?

A sea mist then blocked out the sun, the beach had become of mire,
whilst beautiful sounds came through that mist, reminiscent of a choir,
it drifted o'er the water, so loud and clear when reaching me,
'Oh Lord we ask for help from thee, for those in peril on the sea.'

The mist then cleared to leave the sun, shining oh so bright,
creating a reflection on the water, of a cross of blinding light.
That Holy Cross stopped me in my tracks, I never took another step,
for there beneath my soaking feet; a baby seal trapped in a net.

He was still alive but so distressed, I had to get that little seal free,
and with the aid of broken razor shells, I got him out and back
to the sea.
The hand of God does many things it gave me the right direction,
even though it was a dream; for me it was a wonderful reflection.

Wenn-The-Penn

WHEEL BLISS

A year ago I felt despair when back pain caused intense distress
and closed the door on walking far, for there was no way I could guess
what generosity would bring within the space of twelve months more,
allowing me to seek and find, then go where once I'd been before.
The freedom to do things I choose, to travel anywhere I please,
came with a mode of transport that would pave my way around
                                                                     with ease -
one powered chair on four small wheels, a strange, but great new
                                                                     way of life,
mobility the like of which held no more pain, or stress, or strife.
My seated height has opened doors, enabled me to break new ground;
I find I'm on the best of terms with youngsters that I see around
and converse now with adult folk and children of all ages too.
I'm shown such kindness, offered help with anything I try to do.
I'm quite content, I'm feeling great, I thrive on joviality.
My battery's charged - *oh, ain't life grand* - I've regained
                                                                     lost mobility!

Maureen Atkin

PATHFINDER

Into your hands, oh Lord,
we place this youth.
A child no more, but not yet a man.
Desperately he tries to find his way,
His place, in the big world before him.
He feels the pangs of love, for the first time,
He looks so young.
He rejects the protection of his parents' love,
yet he longs for their care.
While he seeks to fulfil every secret desire,
he is totally oblivious to his parents,
lying awake, restless in the night,
waiting and listening in selfless anxiety,
for his key to turn in the door.
Whatever has gone on now can wait,
the important thing is, that our son
is safely asleep in his own bed.
He came home once again.

Angela Maltby

SOLITUDE

There are many turning points in life:
Shadowy sounds of melancholy music
Drifting from a distance into the soul.
Things tangible are so remote.
A bird in flight above a humming town,
Detached from all reality . . .
Soothed by liquid thought,
Softly rippling on the stony bed of life
Which now can be regarded as a picture,
Calm and unmoving to the passer-by
But to the connoisseur a panorama
Of action, colour, business and the rest,
Each minute detail essential to the whole,
Just as the slightest action
May influence the fate of dynasties -
A pebble thrown haphazard in a pool,
Each far-reaching ripple
Stirring the cool water to its depth -
So, in such contemplation
Is found a sort of peace and consolation,
Spirit renewed, refreshed, revivified,
Reborn in the bracing air above the city,
Again to undertake
The mundane tasks, and therein find some pleasure,
Each new beginning a new turning point,
Based on sure knowledge of an unseen source
Of vitalising faith, and hope, and love.
What more can we need? Thanks be to God.

Maureen Inglis-Taylor

AWARENESS

At break of day I rise and pray
  To God, 'You are so good.
Your care for me, it never fails;
  A perfect Fatherhood.'

At noon of day I pause awhile,
  And think of those at war;
And those who lack what I possess;
  Lives lived; but I ignore.

At evening hour day's work has ceased;
  I vow to do my part.
'Take what I am; all I possess;
  My being and my heart.'

As nightfall comes be this my prayer;
  'No longer mine, but yours.'
For 'Fatherhood' means 'brotherhood';
  We live for love's great cause.

Love's cause is this: that all might know
  God's care for all mankind.
In helping those who need our help,
  Our true selves we will find.

Peter J Millam

THE CROSS

The music of Your silences
Heals my soul.
The visions of Your cross
Are the heartbeats of our God.

My pain You share with me
With tears.
Sweet Jesus, suffer in me,
And let my deaths bring life.

John Rae Walker

WHO AM I?

Who am I but a fleeting cloud,
Blowing across the sky,
Who am I but a blade of grass,
Soon to whither, curl up and die.

Who am I but unknowing and blind,
Unable to see any light,
Who am I but unhearing and deaf,
Unable to hear what is right.

Who am I but a wandering star,
Searching for love, joy and peace,
Who am I but a seeking lost soul,
Looking for blesséd release.

Who am I but a sinner forlorn,
Weak is my frame, and frail,
Who am I but ashes and dust,
All alone I am destined to fail.

Who am I now but a child of God,
I've repented and found the right way,
Who am I now but redeemed and forgiven,
Jesus' blood was the high price to pay.

Who am I now but joyful and free,
Released from sin and shame,
Who am I now but His forever,
Now that I bear His dear name.

Who am I now but a citizen,
In His Kingdom I've found my true home,
Who am I now but His child,
Belovéd and one of His own.

Who am I now but still weak,
But my heart sings a new song,
In Jesus there's victory and power,
So though I am weak, I am strong.

Kerry Ann Watson

KEEP ME TURNING

Turning around - do you see what you expected?
Turn around - what do you see?
Things have changed - have I been away?
Why did I turn, will I stay?

When I turned to look at myself, for who I am,
I learned to love what I had hated,
I learned to love, to appreciate, to enjoy,
Now I wonder of those who can't.

Leaving home - I turned . . .
I was deserted, alone with strangers,
I turned, met new friends, became a part,
Became a one, whose choices are mine.

Which way do I turn now?
Will I get shown the way?
I feel a turn coming on . . .
Do I turn away?

Now I turn, although I don't know where,
Time to turn, move on somewhere,
When will what, or who, or me,
Turn me now - who will be?

Future turning - who will turn to me?
To give themselves, as I give me,
Keep on turning - it's not too late,
Keep me turning - the future's bright.

Felicity S Øen

THE DAY GOD CHANGED ME

Long was I bound with Satan's wicked lies,
Death was my only friend as I wished my life to end,
But God's word shed light upon his web.
Words of truth set me free from his lies,
That day I came to realise God loved me
and I was special in his eyes.

God turned the hate in me to love
my enemies became my friends,
His light lit up the darkness of my heart
I repented and from sin was cleansed;

He took my misery and gave me joy
inner turmoil calmed by His peace,
His forgiveness overwhelmed my being
as guilt lifted I felt relief.

Julie McKenzie

Hope Above

When helpless tears are falling
And darkness holds your heart
The hands of faith will open
And lift you to a brighter start.

When days become a struggle
And nights turn into need
Your shadow of light will wake
And send a magic guiding seed.

When loneliness is at your side
And memories tear your mind
Somebody casts a ray of strength
And a smile of hope you'll find.

When morning is a grey cloud
And words of wisdom fail
The light of heaven will catch you
And let all emotions sail.

When sorrow is on your shoulder
And gloom is at your side
The silver star will guide you
No more feelings then denied.

When life becomes a longing
And no answers are in sight
The hands of faith will reach you
In your peaceful sleep tonight.

Rebecca Punter

CARLOOSE, MY SALVATION

Alone and lost, to Thee I cried
The Saviour's arms were open wide -
He found a partner for my soul -
The love of God then made me whole.

He sent me one to guide the way
To help me when I often stray -
Such gentle care He gives to me
From stress and turmoil sets me free.

In meadows green of long ago
'Twas there I learned to love Him so,
His little cottage was my shrine
Christ came to me with divine.

I surely know the Lord is there
I see His bounty everywhere
The starlight and the morning sky,
Such beauty never passed me by.

Marcella Pellow

THE CLASS OF '86

We the ones who through these hallowed halls have trod
And questioned why
Stand now on the verge of normal existence
Our student lives seem a distant past
As we stride out into the unrealising world
Who amongst us will build the new generation
Are we the people who will take the initiative
Will we change what we can to improve our world
We the Class of '86
What change will our tomorrows bring?

Deborah Pothen

THAT EVENING

It was on that evening in February that we met.
After all that time searching and studying
He was just there all along and I only had to ask.
Praise God that I didn't get too deep with that cult
but I kept an open mind and turned to my Bible.
Yet when the Methodist said, 'Receive the Holy Spirit'
I was really expecting *something* to happen.

But *You* had it all worked out in Your good time.
How you saw my heart was on the right line
to seek the truth about Jesus, Your Son
who is the same now and forever
God, 3 in 1.
And on that evening, I met the three of You.

I made Jesus my Lord and I invited Him in
and that peace entered my heart, that made me want to sing
a new song up to You of love and praise
for depression and addiction departed
never to return since those days
of my new birth.

Then, within two weeks,
I went to my girlfriend's bedroom and began to weep.
I saw You hang there on that cross to set us free
and I felt the fire of The Comforter anoint and flow through me.
For the first time in my life I saw the Devil start to flee.
And I knew You were God and had the victory
on February 4th, 1993.

Philip Trivett

I HAVE FOUND A RANSOM

Faint not
Watch and pray
These words were like rivers in the desert
Making my heart firm as a stone
I lifted up my eyes and looked and lo
The journey was far
Now I am in the middle of the road
The villagers around came to me
They fetched me a little water
I washed my feet
And rested myself under the tree
They again fetched me a morsel of bread
To comfort my heart
After, I passed on
The next day I lifted up my eyes
And saw the place far off
Yea, mansions where my risen Master reigns
Alas, I arrive at the place
He hath gone to prepare for me
I fall at His feet and worship Him
Now at the scent of water, Jesus
Has made me bud
And my new life brings forth
Boughs like a plant
I have called and He hath answered
Of His power towards me
I will cease not to give thanks to my Redeemer
Till He calls me home.

Ebenezer Essuman

VACANT BASEMENT WORKROOM!

A basement workroom became vacant
In the house where my best friend lived,
On the spur of the moment
We decided to offer a bid,
Joy! It was accepted!

Hardest part racking our brains to deduce
Some handmade articles to sell,
After office hours produce,
Judged three items suitable to dwell,
Make all; find which would gel.

Jumped into the unknown unafraid
The onset of working non-stop.
Partner found outlets to trade,
Nightly slavish members in sweatshop,
Finish must be tip-top!

Leisure, social times took a back seat,
Holidays became overlooked,
Gradually, we did unseat
Rivals, built up a large order book
As more buyers we hooked.

One at a time we left our employment
Enlarged, employed more staff ourselves
All challenging enjoyment
Bidding to export, fill Britain's shelves;
Premises accumulative.

We've loved every up and down second,
Diversified, expanded *vroom!*
Chance comment opened scene to green lands,
Lives budded then burst into full bloom
From vacant basement workroom!

Hilary Jill Robson

THE ECHO

Now as I stand in the depths of my winter
Reviewing the journey from whence it begun,
I feel all the love in my heart in an echo
Of days now long-gone, when I stood in the sun.

Far over space, beyond reach of rainbows
Winging through galaxies - twinkling star,
There beats the echo of what was once all of me
There in embrace, my loving arms are.

Now you must touch me before I am gone from you
Always to know where happiness is,
For then like the seashell, the echo is part of you
Sweet as eternity's lingering kiss.

I look to the sky and hear the child's laughter,
My hair takes the wind which caresses my face,
My tongue catches raindrops, my heart joins the birdsong
With stardust in moonlight I go from this place.

My life is my love and lives ever onward
The hard days now over, the joys yet to come,
My echo of love will always be here with you
The echo of days, when I stood in the sun.

Alison Forbes

I'D REALLY LIKE TO LOVE YOU, LORD

'I'd really like to love You, Lord,
But O my heart is sore!
So many disappointments have
Depressed me more and more!

I've tried to trust You, Lord, it's true,
But then disaster strikes -
You ask so much of all Your friends,
No wonder no-one likes

To stick their neck out and proclaim,
Jesus is always there -
Sometimes I even wonder if
You really see or care.

And then I think of Your great love
And all that You went through,
And how You yearned to save and heal -
That love includes me too.

You really understand my woes,
Of that I have no doubt,
So dare I listen to Your voice?
Please come and sort me out.'

That prayer was answered in a flash,
He helped me start to climb.
I'll not look back, I'm on the way,
He's with me all the time.

Peter Spurgin

IN MY HEART

You have redeemed my mind
Which has lead me to find
Freedom when thinking about Your love
When coming into this world
In setting free, sinners like me.

Chorus:
In my heart
Feelings are growing strong
In my heart
You gave me a blessing
In cleansing my heart.

You have cleansed my soul
Which was like burning coal
And nearly led me to fall
Into hell's hot coals
But now scored too many goals.

Chorus

You have freed my spirit
Which has directed me
To the Light You're shining
Around the world
And deep within my soul.

Austin Satz

INTO THE BEAUTIFUL LIGHT OF HEAVEN

They had been taunting me for three years -
the voices of the mind: so very real, but not there
in reality. I saw the ropes, coffins, wheeled biers
which their unremitting chorus caused such fear
within me that I tried to destroy myself - to kill them.
I went through the motions to retain a glimmer
of my faith: thought of her who caught at the hem
of Christ's cloak, He came to heal the sick, the sinner.

Voices, sounds, sights - manifestations of an illness,
a psychosis and with depression bound my soul
in tight enclosure which would lead to the stillness
of death unless I could find an escape, a small hole
through which to crawl from the deep circles of a hell.
I did not have Virgil as my guide but my caring wife.
Therapies, treatments, medications: no difference tell,
I was locked into a low orbit of a just functioning life.

There was no sudden point or moment of release
from the vaulted tomb of the psychosis, but rather
confluence of man's research and God's love - real ease
came: new generation drug and the aid of the Mother
of our Lord. From darkness I slowly emerged into
the gentling light not of Heaven but of the real day
of the living, it was as if on Everest's peak - air too thin to
shout but to God, wife, scientist, doctor, priest, 'Thanks' I pray.

Andrew Duncan

Turn Around - Dick Whittington

Your hands bear all the marks of absent wealth,
The scars of heavy toil and hours spent,
For meagre pay; and yet with spirit bent,
You crawl away from London town. With stealth
You leave the pavements lined with silver and with gold,
Slinking down the Strand as though you're through,
Without your cat.
        Change tack.
              Turn back.
                   Listen to
The change which bells of Bow have thrice foretold.

What message do these ancient Bow bells bring?
Turn back, turn back, just listen to these chimes,
Turn back, three times Lord Mayor, three times, three times.
He laughs and throws his hat into the ring.

With a spring in his gait he returns to his fate,
To the smart pin-stripes of Threadneedle Street,
Only to learn that his cat has been sold to meet,
The appetites of creditors too lean to wait.

He commences his election campaign,
Calling upon the mighty and the meek,
To rise and let their noble city speak
For him. But all his efforts prove to be in vain.

With peels of laughter the bells of Bow burst into song,
Ding dong, ding dong, we're very sorry we were wrong.

Temple Bar, The Thames, without votes, all-in,
Sitting speechless in the smog on elbowed knee,
Watching the river roll by to the sea.
But then warm feline fur against rough skin.

He throws his battered hat into the air.
It's back to his rural roots, with injured pride,
But friendship and loyalty by his side,
Leaving the city to induct its new Lord Mayor.

A K S

THE HANDOVER

My life was a mess,
a muddle of confusion and hurt
where fear reigned supreme
with hate its faithful lackey
in a dismal existence
where 'shoulder-chips' filled a hod.

I was, at the best,
a sarcastic cynic who would blurt
out remarks I deemed
amusing - yet were tacky -
in determined persistence
to hide *my* complexes . . . *clod!*

Then suddenly blessed
with the grace which had patiently lurked,
as if in a dream
I saw colours, not khaki;
dropping inane resistance,
I put my faith in God!

Eve O Lucién

Healing Wings

When I am broken and in despair
Crushed, in anguish - no one cares:
I lift my eyes to Calvary
And see the One who died for me.

My spirit then begins to rise
I turn for healing - am I surprised?
Your eyes of compassion look at me,
'I'll give you peace, I'll set you free!'

'Receive your healing in My Name -
'Tis for your freedom that I came.
Accept the joy My Spirit brings
With healing power in My wings'

'O Lord, I turn my heart to You:
My soul, my life I give anew.
I claim my healing in Your Name.
Lord Jesus, have Your way and reign'

Christine Rutherford

THE LETTER

The turning point in my life
Was one of unexpected joy
When I received a letter bringing
News of my long-lost boy -
A darling little child, cruelly lost -
My son, that I gave up to another,
Forced from my loving arms,
Separated from his birth mother.
Long years of soulful yearning
Now filled with expectancy
As he travels down to meet me
To be united, emotionally.
All the years of regretting finished
An ending to great strife
Torment over, inherent love rekindled
At a turning point in life.

P R McDonald

I Am No Fool

A full twenty years have passed since I did leave school,
Have proved to myself and others, I am no fool.
For I have obtained an English Honours degree,
Results arrived, it was the turning point for me.

And my results were much better than I had thought,
Justifying the champagne my spouse bought.
Seeing my degree certificate fills me with pride,
Often caught glancing at it with smile I can't hide.

Susan Mullinger

STORMS

An accidental journey,
a sold out cinema show,
an inexplicable course of events
that made me stay
- and a strange uncertain feeling
that made me wait for you.

One look, a fatal glimpse,
can cause untold disruption.
But for the pain,
the long-lost hours of uncertainty and separation
of resignation and, perhaps, disappointment,
for rejection or misery;
For one night
I would trade years of these storms.
One night made my memories whole
the ever embedded thoughts
that only two can know
 - and I the one.

So I love the pain
as I loved the night.
For without the pain,
the pleasure ne'er would be so pure.
And I wait,
and pray,
that I may hurt again.

J S Elliott

GOLDEN YEARS

Fifty years have come and gone,
We're still together still 'as one',
We've had our 'ups' we've had our 'downs',
Our laughter, tears, our smiles our frowns,

And there were times I must admit,
It seemed I couldn't cope with it,
When things went wrong and tempers frayed,
I got down on my knees and prayed

And asked the Lord to guide us,
All along the way,
He walked the road beside us,
He is our strength and stay.

I'm glad I stayed the course with you,
We've proved that love can see us through,
For love is strong and love is true,
I wouldn't change a day would you?

And now I think we'll drink a toast,
To love that never ends,
We've reached our golden milestone,
And stayed the 'best of friends'.

Mary G Kane

TURNING POINT

Be positive now,
Don't look back;
Give all the
Negatives the sack!
You've moved forward
Towards your goal,
And mending for good
Your damaged soul.

You've struggled on
For three long years;
Working through
Multitudinous fears,
Forcing painful memories
Right to the fore,
Memories suppressed
From years of yore,
Healing those hurts
That damaged your teens,
Hurts and abuse
That should never have been.

Now . . . realisation
That you can be whole,
That no-one can ever
Possess your soul;
Counselling has enabled
You to say,
That in the future,
Come what may,
With all the help
You have received,
And all the strategies
You have perceived,

You'll be able to cope
And on self rely,
All the rest of your life,
Till the day that you die.

J D Reeve

WHEN YOU CAME INTO MY LIFE

When you came into my life
You brought with you a smile
That I will never forget,
Always laughing
Always joking
I still remember the day
That we first met,
You teased and made fun
And we had some laughs
But it took you a while
Until you asked.
I was so nervous
And embarrassed too
But I was glad
To be asked out by you.
A lot has changed
In this past year
Now to the alter
Is the way we steer,
We both have rings
As a symbol of our love
You've changed my world
For the better
And for good.

Caroline Amess

THE DAY I MET HIM

I sat alone filled with despair
Depressed and sad, did anyone care?
No-one to turn to nowhere to go
What to do I did not know

From the highest hill I wanted to shout
Tell me what's this life about
I dropped to my knees and I did say
'Help me God is what I pray.'

He heard my prayer He heard my cry
Suddenly I wanted to live not die
And to my Bible I was led
Accept God's Son is what it said

I asked Him to be my Saviour that day
And new life started straight away
He took away every bit of sadness
And replaced it with a life of gladness

Problems they can still be there
But no more do I despair
Because His gentle voice I hear
And the problems they all disappear

He's changed my life in every way
I'm glad He heard my prayer that day
He's set me free from a life so grim
I bless the day that I met Him

Janet McBride

LIFELINE

0345 90 90 90 . . .

Finger hovered, dipped, then dialled,
Listened - with an erratic heart -
To a voice of silk, béchamel distilled,
Quieting my thuds of apprehension.

Once explained, as comprehensively
As I could with such faltering,
There were no soporific answers,
Only tacit understanding.

From stunned lips, these depths
Of extreme confession sounded as
Another's explanations, I could never
Be so blatantly wicked.

When asked how old
I might conceivably be,
I answered, 'As old as time itself,
Or as young as human love.'

In the expansion of a smile,
I was, with humour, accepted
For what I am - no sinner, just frail human.
My lifeline . . .

0345 90 90 90

David Bramley

EARLY MORNING PRAYER

I set my clock for six one day,
For at six-thirty we would pray

A prayer meeting it was to be,
But no-one turned up - only me

Twice this happened, and then again
This was how me The Lord did train

To get up early in the day
So before breakfast I could pray

And as a habit it became
I began to praise Jesu's Name

As early I sought Him each day
I found He helped me on my way

Thus I sought Him through the years
He helped me in my joys and fears

And Jesus Christ still thrills me so
Though now to church I cannot go

Since in those early years I'd known
How to come to Jesus alone

P Rock

THE DAY I CROSSED MY RIVER, AND CHANGED MY LIFE

One day I came to a river so deep
Looked around at its banks so steep
Paused awhile, looked everywhere
Felt a presence of someone near
Looked around felt a surge
Of strength, of joy, but mostly love
Thought about this life I am living
Not all good, often need forgiving
Looked at the river its banks so steep
Now I must cross it if I am to keep
This feeling of peace, of joy, of love,
I know is a message from *God* above
So down the bank of the river I go
Into the water that will cleanse my soul
When I leave this river and climb ashore
I know I've become a Christian once more
For the river I saw was life's crossroads for me
And now I have crossed it in *Christ* will I be.

Maureen Smith

THE TURNING POINT

A touch, a look, a certain smile,
An ordinary phrase, effect extraordinary,
A burst of light suffused my eyes,
An everyday man becomes a guide;
Although he speaks of this and that,
A matter only of a daily life,
And now this ordinary life is rearranged,
A landscape changed, forever bright,
A burden lifted, air uplifted,
A turning point transforms my life.

Carnela Carr

PATERNAL PRIDE
(A turning point, from remembered yesterdays)

He gets in and sinks into the big seat beside me,
Prays with paired hands held high-on-head, ties
His shawl turban-wise, closes the door carefully,

And seems to see nothing beyond the dashboard
As I drive on, save the portentous radiator-cap's
Shining tip, standing upright, pointing skyward.

Why would he want to, when all his world is inside
This huge car? His bronze body puffing with pride,
Eyes roving all over me, sighing he mumbles, 'Son,

How so happy I am, that my promise I have kept
To my lost brother, your loving father. Childless
To be God made me, but it was my joy to accept

You, starting today as an engineer, with your own
Chariot-like car and a self-earned licence to drive.
Now, please, Son, drop me on your way to town,

Near the gate of that only-other-guy owning a car
Over here, who didn't bother to teach you to drive
Though I had beseeched him several times so far.'

I had to blink so hard and tight
To see ahead and steer straight,
With the sun too blessing bright.

Kopan Mahadeva

A New Beginning

It took a while,
It didn't happen overnight.
But it happened, and that's what matters -
I changed. I became a different person,
A much more . . . in control person - only I . . . know.

Almost gone is the old me -
The one so easily affected
By life's negative side.
The quick-tempered one, the intolerant one,
The selfish, so selfish one . . .
The vulnerable old me - almost gone.
I am learning to love. Now life's
Suddenly beautiful. And I
Am in control
Of me. A much more . . . in control person -
Only I . . . know. The author
Of my own unhappiness, I was.
I one day understood -
One can choose to be happy.

And here I am
What I am
A much more . . . in control person -
Dealing with different sides of me.
Making the choice.

Claire-Lyse Sylvester

VILLANELLE FOR A RETURN

As through grey wind and slanting rain we came
to see and sense the place where I was born,
memories had faded, nothing stays the same.

We trod forgotten cobbles, felt the shame
of ruined buildings in this town forlorn,
as through grey wind and slanting rain we came.

Each square, each street, each block had changed its name.
Our language lost for childhood days to mourn;
memories had faded, nothing stays the same.

The suburb now so green and flat and tame
belied the dreadful violence it had worn,
as through grey wind and slanting rain we came.

Transplanted here another people claim
new roots, new hearth, new hedge of sharp hawthorn.
Memories had faded, nothing stays the same.

Decades ago we fled by westbound train -
so now, but willing, and to a chosen home;
as through grey wind and slanting rain we came,
memories had faded, nothing stays the same.

Marianne Hellwig John

TURNING POINT

The pain I suffered after the fall -
Was so painful - I couldn't dance at the ball -
I could not walk so very far -
But one day I walked into a coffee bar,
Started talking to a lady and she gave me a remedy.

She said 'Take cod liver oil and orange juice each day'
She was right, in time it took the pain away!
'You must take it every morning without fail' she said
'As soon as you get out of bed.
Soon you will walk without your stick - and you'll
    walk quick again, ever so slick.'

'You will dance again, but it will take a while
until you get back to your normal style,
so take advice from one who knows -
persevere - do not give in, and then you may
enter a marathon race - and *win!*'

You came into my life that day - then you left
so we had little time to know each other more -
but your advice I took and the remedy worked well -
I walked again, and then I could dance with the men -
went along my own same self, but I would love to have
met you once more after you had left through the
coffee bar door -
to tell you of the turning point in my life then -
about your remedy - it could have helped so many!

M E Smith

My Everything

The letterbox rattled, I rushed to the door
Saw the face of *my Lord* looking up from the floor.
His hair was dishevelled, His kind eyes looked worn
Blood flowed down His face where the thorn crown had torn.
As I picked up the card, these words met my eye
'Is it *nothing* to you, all ye that pass by?'
'It means a great deal' - protesting, I blamed
That secret questioner - then I was shamed!
Looked again at the One who had given His *all*
Born such pain for *me!* - Should He now on me call
For *less* than my *everything* in loving care
Through Him to His children for whom He hung there?
I never have known just who made that call
Challenging full commitment - nothing less than my *all*
But I bless the day when they troubled to bring
That face of the Crucified - face of my King!

Mavis Brett

INFORMATION

We hope you have enjoyed reading this book - and that you will continue to enjoy it in the coming years.

If you like reading and writing poetry drop us a line, or give us a call, and we'll send you a free information pack.

Write to :-
**Triumph House Information
1-2 Wainman Road
Woodston
Peterborough
PE2 7BU
(01733) 230749**